SPIN AND THE FLASH DRIVE

Written by Aspen Ham

Illustrated by Katie Williams

IT WAS A PERFECT 67 DEGREES OUTSIDE. THE SUN WAS SHINING RIGHT THROUGH THE CLOUDS ONTO SPIN'S FACE.

HE STEPPED OUT OF HIS FRONT DOOR, READY FOR SCHOOL, NOT REALIZING THIS WOULD BE A DAY HE WOULD NEVER FORGET.

"Spin and the Flash Drive" was created in partnership with Prevention Specialist Anthony Tidwell. Mr. Tidwell is a dedicated Prevention Specialist and the visionary founder of Cutwell4Kids, an organization committed to nurturing the well-being and growth of children. With a profound sense of purpose, he has made it his life's mission to reduce and prevent substance abuse, focusing on proactive outreach, education, and support within communities. Through Cutwell4Kids, Anthony empowers youth by providing them with creative outlets and resources that encourage personal development and resilience. His impactful work continues to inspire change, fostering healthier and more hopeful futures for young individuals.

PRESS & DESIGN
KA

THE BIRDS WERE CHIRPING, CARS WERE PASSING BY. IT WAS A TYPICAL MORNING IN SANTA CRUZ.

HE REACHED BACK BEHIND HIM FOR HIS SKATEBOARD, TOSSED IT DOWN ON THE GROUND AND JUMPED ON. HE WAS HEADING DOWN THE HILL ON HIS WAY TO SCHOOL.

"MORNING, ZACK," SPIN YELLED, RAISING HIS HAND HIGH IN THE AIR AS HE ROLLED UP TO SCHOOL. SPIN FLIPPED HIS SKATEBOARD UP WITH HIS FOOT, CATCHING IT IN THE AIR, AND TUCKED IT UNDER HIS ARM.

ZACK AND SPIN HAVE BEEN BEST FRIENDS SINCE 1ST GRADE AND MEET UP EVERY MORNING BEFORE THE BELL RINGS.

2 HOURS LATER....

SPIN WAS STARING AT THE CLOCK TRYING TO FOCUS, BUT HE KNEW RECESS WAS JUST SECONDS AWAY. SPIN GLANCED AT THE CLOCK, FEELING EVERY SECOND STRETCH. IT FELT LIKE AN ETERNITY AS HE WAITED FOR THE BELL TO RING.

SPIN AND ZACK FLEW OUT OF THEIR SEATS AND RACED OUT THE DOOR TO THE PLAYGROUND.

IT WAS JUST ONE OF THOSE DAYS THAT WAS TOO NICE TO WASTE SITTING INSIDE.

THE OUTSIDE DOOR SLAMMED BEHIND THE CLASS JUST AS THE BREEZE PUSHED IT CLOSED. THE BOYS KEPT RUNNING PAST THE MONKEY BARS. THEY BOTH RACED TO THE FOOTBALL LYING BY THE FENCE.

IT WASN'T LONG BEFORE LOTS OF THEIR CLASSMATES JOINED THEM TO PLAY. THEY STOOD HUDDLED TOGETHER TRYING TO DECIDE WHO WOULD GET TO THROW FIRST. AFTER MUCH DELIBERATION, THEY AGREED THAT ZACK COULD THROW FIRST SINCE HIS BIRTHDAY WAS SATURDAY.

THE GROUP OF BOYS RACED TO THE OPPOSITE SIDE OF ZACK. AS SPIN WAS RUNNING, HE HEARD A CRUNCH UNDERNEATH HIS FEET. HE LOOKED DOWN AND FOUND A SMALL BLACK OBJECT WITH A CAP ON IT. HE PICKED IT UP, PUT IT IN HIS POCKET, AND RAN OVER TO THE REST OF HIS FRIENDS, EAGER TO BE THE FIRST ONE TO CATCH THE BALL.

"THROW IT, THROW IT!" THEY CHANTED.

TODAY WAS THURSDAY, WHICH MEANT THAT AFTER RECESS, SPIN'S CLASS WENT TO TECHNOLOGY. THIS WEEK THEY WERE WORKING AT STATIONS, ROTATING BETWEEN THE 3D PRINTERS AND CODING. SOMEHOW, SPIN CONVINCED THE TEACHER TO PUT HIM AND ZACK TOGETHER IN A GROUP.

"YESSSSSS!" SPIN AND ZACK EXCLAIMED WHEN THEY HEARD THEY GOT TO WORK TOGETHER.

Daily Schedule

8:00am Calendar
8:15am Math
9:45am Reading
11:00am Recess
11:30 History
12:00pm Lunch
12:30pm Recess
1:00pm Technology
2:00pm Science
3:00pm Dismissal

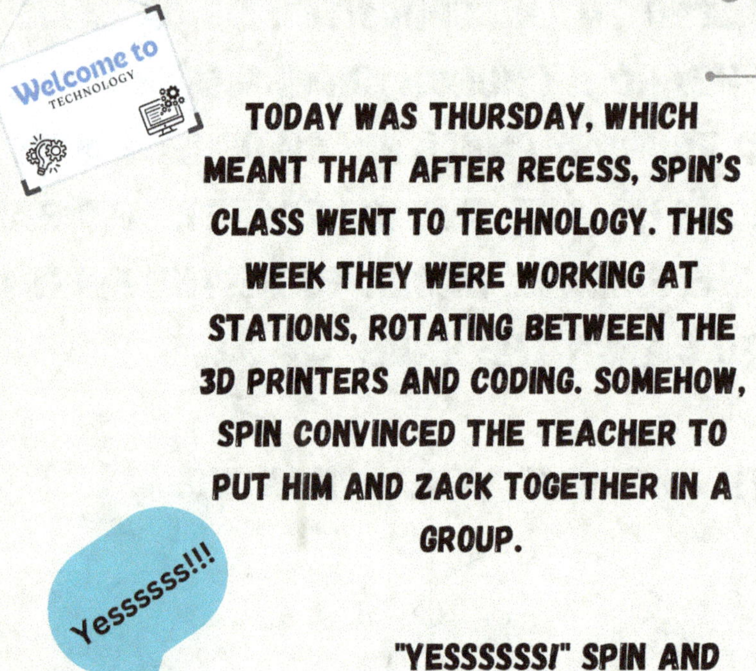

THEY WERE SO EXCITED UNTIL THEY FOUND OUT THE NEW BOY WAS ALSO IN THEIR GROUP. HE HAD JUST MOVED FROM A SMALL MOUNTAIN TOWN IN WASHINGTON.

IT WAS WALLY'S 3RD DAY OF SCHOOL AND HE WAS YET TO SAY A SINGLE WORD TO ANYONE OTHER THAN THE TEACHER.

WHILE THE OTHER GROUP ACROSS THE ROOM WAS GETTING HELP WITH THE 3D PRINTER, SPIN PULLED OUT THE STRANGE BLACK OBJECT FROM HIS POCKET.

"OOOO, WHAT DO YOU THINK MIGHT BE ON IT?" SAID SPIN. "MAYBE THERE IS TOP SECRET INFORMATION ON THERE," CHUCKLED ZACK.

SPIN TOOK OFF THE CAP AND TRIED TO PLUG IT INTO THE COMPUTER, BUT THE FLASH DRIVE WOULDN'T FIT INTO ANY PORT. THE BOYS LOOKED AT EACH OTHER, CONFUSED.

"NO WAY!" HOLLERED SPIN.

"SHHH," SAID ZACK. "YOU'RE GOING TO GET US IN TROUBLE FOR BEING LOUD!"

ZACK AND SPIN LOOKED AT EACH OTHER IN COMPLETE DISMAY, BOTH BECAUSE WALLY FINALLY SPOKE AND BECAUSE HE SAID THE OBJECT WAS A VAPE.

"A VAPE?" ZACK SAID, HIS EYES WIDE. "HOW DO YOU KNOW IT'S A VAPE?"

WALLY GOT QUIET AND STARED AT HIS SHOES, UNWILLING TO MAKE EYE CONTACT WITH THE OTHER TWO BOYS. "BECAUSE AFTER MY BROTHER ENDED UP IN THE HOSPITAL IN A COMA, MY PARENTS FOUND TONS OF THOSE UNDER HIS BED."

SPIN'S EYES WIDENED. HE TRIED HIS BEST TO SECRETLY SHOVE THE VAPE BACK INTO HIS POCKET WHERE MR. ROSE WOULDN'T SEE AND PROMPTLY PLACED HIS HANDS BACK ON THE KEYBOARD.

"YES, SIR," THEY ANSWERED, AND GOT BACK TO WORK.

A FEW MINUTES LATER, MR. ROSE WAS BACK ON THE OTHER SIDE OF THE CLASSROOM HELPING SOME OTHER STUDENTS WITH THEIR WORK. "YOU HAVE TO GIVE THAT TO AN ADULT", WALLY MUTTERED UNDER HIS BREATH. "IT'S DANGEROUS". "IT CAN'T BE THAT BIG OF A DEAL", WHISPERED ZACK. "I SEE TONS OF HIGH SCHOOL KIDS WITH THEM IN THE BATHROOMS AT THE FOOTBALL GAMES".

WALLY SIGHED, "I DIDN'T THINK IT WAS THAT BIG OF A DEAL EITHER. I SAW MY BROTHER WITH IT AND HE TOLD ME NOT TO TELL. HE HAS ALWAYS BEEN THERE FOR ME AND TAKEN CARE OF ME WHEN MY PARENTS WORK LATE. I TRUSTED HIM. HE TOLD ME HE WOULD GET ME ONE AND WE COULD HANG OUT IF I KEPT IT A SECRET. THE NEXT DAY HE PASSED OUT IN THE SCHOOL BATHROOM AND WENT INTO A COMA. I WILL NEVER FORGET SEEING HIM IN THE HOSPITAL LIKE THAT. IT WAS TWO MONTHS BEFORE HE COULD COME HOME. THE DOCTORS SAID HE CAN'T EVEN PLAY SPORTS ANYMORE BECAUSE HIS LUNGS ARE SO DAMAGED. MY PARENTS DIDN'T EVEN KNOW HE WAS VAPING".

SPIN PUT HIS HAND IN HIS POCKET, MAKING SURE THE VAPE WAS STILL THERE. HE WAS SHAKING. IN THAT MOMENT, SPIN STARTED THINKING ABOUT HIS LITTLE BROTHER, WHO WAS ONLY TWO. HE COULDN'T IMAGINE BEING IN A COMA AND MISSING TWO MONTHS OF HIS LIFE. SURE, SOMETIMES HIS LITTLE BROTHER CRIED AND PULLED ON HIS HAIR, BUT SPIN COULDN'T IMAGINE ASKING HIM TO COVER LIKE THAT. SUDDENLY, A WAVE OF EMOTIONS CAME OVER SPIN. WITH HIS HEART POUNDING, HE MADE UP HIS MIND. HE RAISED HIS HAND, DETERMINED TO DO THE RIGHT THING.

"MR. ROSE!" SPIN SHOUTED AS HE RAISED HIS HAND. "I NEED TO SPEAK WITH YOU; IT IS REALLY IMPORTANT."

"UHH, OK SPIN, STEP INTO THE HALL AND I WILL BE RIGHT THERE," SAID MR. ROSE. "EVERYONE RETURN TO YOUR SEAT AND WORK ON THE TYPING LESSON POSTED". CONFUSED, MR. ROSE PROCEEDED TO WHERE SPIN WAS STANDING. "WHAT'S UP, SPIN?" SAID MR. ROSE.

SPIN STUCK HIS HAND IN HIS POCKET AND PULLED OUT THE VAPE. HE WAS SICK TO HIS STOMACH. HE COULD SEE ZACK AND WALLY WATCHING FROM THEIR SEATS. HE FROZE, STANDING SILENT. ALL HE COULD THINK ABOUT WAS HIS LITTLE BROTHER.

"OH MY, SPIN, WHERE DID YOU GET THIS?" SAID MR. ROSE.

STUTTERING, SPIN SAID, "ON THE FIELD... DURING RECESS. I'M SORRY, I SHOULD HAVE TURNED IT IN RIGHT AWAY. I THOUGHT IT WAS A FLASH DRIVE."

"YOU DID THE RIGHT THING TURNING IT IN," HE SAID. "I APPRECIATE YOUR HONESTY. YOU KNOW THE ONLY THING YOU SHOULD EVER BREATHE IS CLEAN AIR."

"YES SIR", SPIN SAID. HE WENT BACK INTO THE CLASSROOM AND TOOK HIS SEAT. TRYING TO FOCUS AND NOT THINK ABOUT WHAT JUST HAPPENED, SPIN SAT QUIETLY AND TRIED TO FINISH HIS TYPING LESSON. NONE OF THE BOYS BROUGHT IT BACK UP AGAIN THAT CLASS. IN FACT THEY DIDN'T TALK ANY MORE THE REST OF TECHNOLOGY.

THAT NIGHT, WHEN SPIN SAT DOWN TO DINNER, HE DIDN'T COMPLAIN ONE BIT WHEN HIS LITTLE BROTHER TOMMY INSISTED ON SITTING NEXT TO HIM.

SPIN WAS HAPPY TO BE HOME AFTER SUCH A LONG DAY.

AFTER THE SUN WENT DOWN AND IT WAS TIME FOR BED, SPIN PUT ON HIS PJS AND BRUSHED HIS TEETH. HE CLIMBED INTO HIS BED AND PULLED UP THE COVERS. AFTER HIS MOM KISSED HIM GOOD NIGHT AND TURNED OUT HIS LIGHT, SPIN CLOSED HIS EYES.

HE FLASHED BACK TO HIS CONVERSATION FROM EARLIER TODAY WITH WALLY, AND HIS EYES OPENED WIDE. ALL HE COULD THINK ABOUT WAS HOW SCARED HE MUST HAVE FELT WHILE HIS BROTHER WAS UNCONSCIOUS IN THE HOSPITAL. IT WAS THEN THAT SPIN MADE A PROMISE TO HIMSELF: TO NEVER VAPE AND TO STAND UP FOR WHAT IS RIGHT. HE CLOSED HIS EYES, TURNED OVER, AND FELL FAST ASLEEP. TODAY WAS A DAY HE WOULD NEVER FORGET.

THE END.

About the Illustrator

Katie Williams earned her B.S. in Education from Henderson State University and her M.S. in Information Technology from Arkansas Tech University. She is a Computer Science and Game Design Teacher in Arkansas, has a deep love for graphic design. Katie eagerly embraced the challenge to illustrate "Spin and the Flash Drive," bringing Spin and his friends to life through vivid and engaging artwork. A mother of 4 children, Katie feels strongly about the risk of vaping among youth. This book is Katie's debut as an illustrator, showcasing her talent and enthusiasm for creative design.

About the Author

Aspen Ham graduated from The University of Texas at Arlington with her B.S. in Early Childhood Education. In the last few years she has also earned her M.S.E. in Technology Leadership and EdS. in Curriculum Leadership from Henderson State University. Aspen is an EAST Facilitator in Arkansas, passionate about educating young minds. Witnessing the harmful effects of nicotine on family members, Aspen feels a strong responsibility to address the serious issue of smoking and vaping. As a parent, this mission has become even more personal, driving the creation of "Spin and the Flash Drive" to help prevent young children from engaging in such dangerous habits.